CAMBRIDGE
Primary English

Phonics Workbook A

Gill Budgell & Kate Ruttle

My name is ....

I am .... years old.

I go to ....

.... School.

Shaftesbury Road, Cambridge CB2 8EA, United Kingdom

One Liberty Plaza, 20th Floor, New York, NY 10006, USA

477 Williamstown Road, Port Melbourne, VIC 3207, Australia

314–321, 3rd Floor, Plot 3, Splendor Forum, Jasola District Centre, New Delhi – 110025, India

103 Penang Road, #05–06/07, Visioncrest Commercial, Singapore 238467

Cambridge University Press & Assessment is a department of the University of Cambridge.

We share the University's mission to contribute to society through the pursuit of education, learning and research at the highest international levels of excellence.

www.cambridge.org
Information on this title: www.cambridge.org/9781108789950

© Cambridge University Press & Assessment 2021

This publication is in copyright. Subject to statutory exception and to the provisions of relevant collective licensing agreements, no reproduction of any part may take place without the written permission of Cambridge University Press & Assessment.

First published 2015
Second edition 2021

20 19 18 17 16 15 14 13 12 11 10 9 8 7 6 5

Printed in the Netherlands by Wilco BV

A catalogue record for this publication is available from the British Library

ISBN 978-1-108-78995-0 Paperback with digital access (1 Year)

Cambridge University Press & Assessment has no responsibility for the persistence or accuracy of URLs for external or third-party internet websites referred to in this publication and does not guarantee that any content on such websites is, or will remain, accurate or appropriate. Information regarding prices, travel timetables, and other factual information given in this work is correct at the time of first printing but Cambridge University Press & Assessment does not guarantee the accuracy of such information thereafter.

....

NOTICE TO TEACHERS IN THE UK
It is illegal to reproduce any part of this work in material form (including photocopying and electronic storage) except under the following circumstances:
(i) where you are abiding by a licence granted to your school or institution by the Copyright Licensing Agency;
(ii) where no such licence exists, or where you wish to exceed the terms of a licence, and you have gained the written permission of Cambridge University Press & Assessment;
(iii) where you are allowed to reproduce without permission under the provisions of Chapter 3 of the Copyright, Designs and Patents Act 1988, which covers, for example, the reproduction of short passages within certain types of educational anthology and reproduction for the purposes of setting examination questions.

Cover image by Pablo Gallego (Beehive Illustration)
Image on p.19: Magnilion/Getty Images.

Contents

Page	Letters and sounds	Templates
4–5	Rhyming words	1
6–7	Words that start with the same letter sound	2
8–9	**s** (sad) and **a** (ant)	1
10–11	**t** (tin) and **n** (net)	4
12–13	**i** (in) and **p** (pan)	2
14–15	Look back	3
16–17	**o** (on), **g** (gum) and **d** (dad)	4
18–19	**m** (mum), **c** (cat) and **k** (kit)	5
20–21	**r** (run), **e** (egg) and **u** (up)	1
22–23	Look back	6
24–25	**h** (hat), **b** (bat), **l** (leg) and **f** (fun)	5
26–27	Double letters: **ck** (sack), **ll** (hill), **ff** (puff), **ss** (miss)	4
28–29	**j** (jug), **v** (van), **w** (win) and **x** (box)	2
30–31	**y** (yawn), **z** (zoo), **zz** (buzz) and **qu** (quick)	2, 3
32–33	Look back	3
34–35	Adjacent consonants	6
36–37	**ng** (sing), **nk** (bank) and **th** (this, thin)	2, 5
38–39	**sh** (ship) and **ch** (chin)	1
40–41	**ai** (wait), **ee** (feet)	4
42–43	**ie** (pie) and **oa** (boat)	6
44–45	**long oo** (boot) and **short oo** (foot)	2, 6
46–47	Look back	2, 5
48–49	**ar** (car), or (fork), **ir** (bird) and **er** (her)	4
50–51	**ow** (cow) and **oi** (coin)	5
52–53	**ear** (hear) and **air** (hair)	2
54–55	Look back	3
56–64	Teaching phonics using Phonics Workbook A	

Template 1

Circle three things in the picture that rhyme with  cat.

Draw things that rhyme with  hen.

Rhyming words

Find pairs of rhyming pictures.
Colour each pair in the same colour.

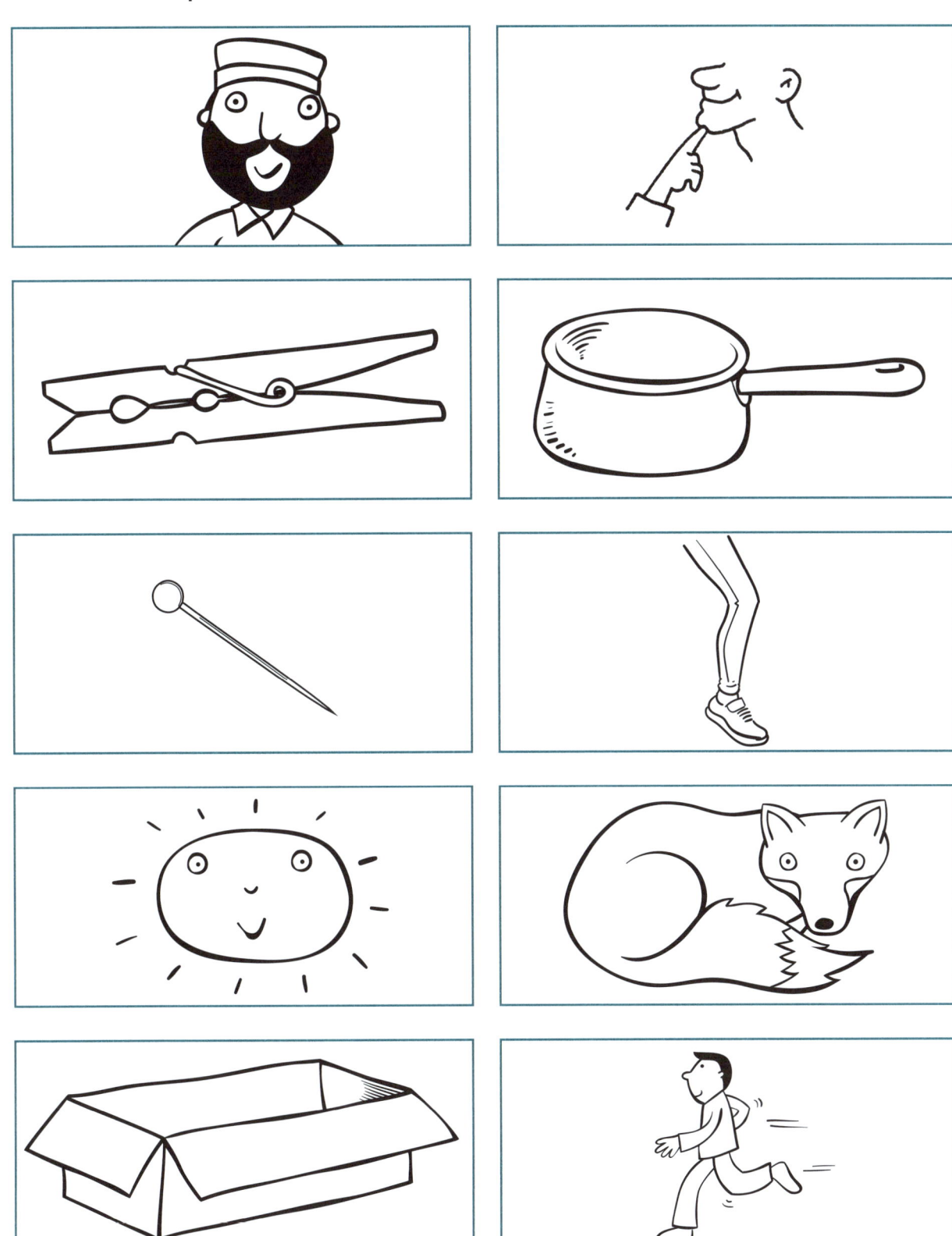

Template 2

Say the words for the pictures.

Join pictures of words that **begin** with the same sound.

6

Words that start with the same letter sound

Draw the tiger's tail through all the pictures of things that begin with the same letter sound t.

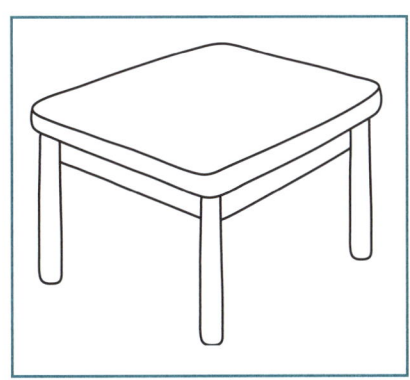

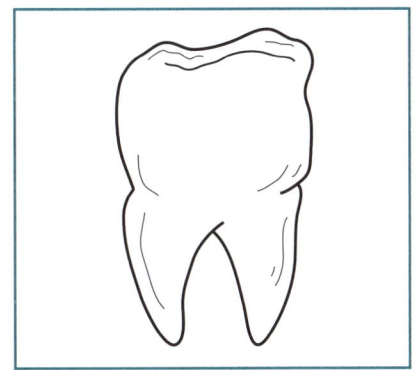

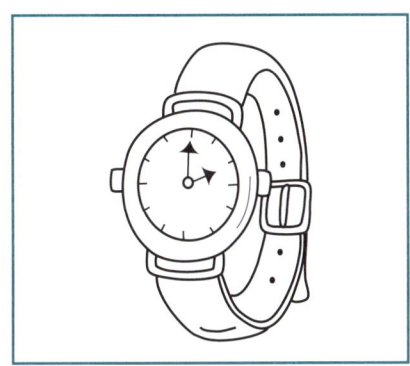

Draw something that begins with t.

Template 1

Trace the letter and say the sound.

S   S   S   S   S   S

Circle the things that begin with the sound **s**.

Draw two more things that begin with **s**. Write **s** next to them.

s and a

Trace the letter and say the sound.

a a a a a a

Write **a** next to pictures of things that begin with the sound **a**.
Colour them.

Read and trace the word **as**.

as   as   as

Circle the word **as** in the sentence.

Anjit is as active as an ant.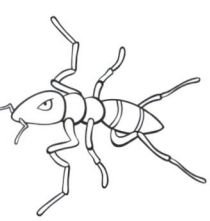

9

Template 4

Trace the letter and say the sound.

t   t   t   t   t   t

Say the words. Write the letter for the first sound.

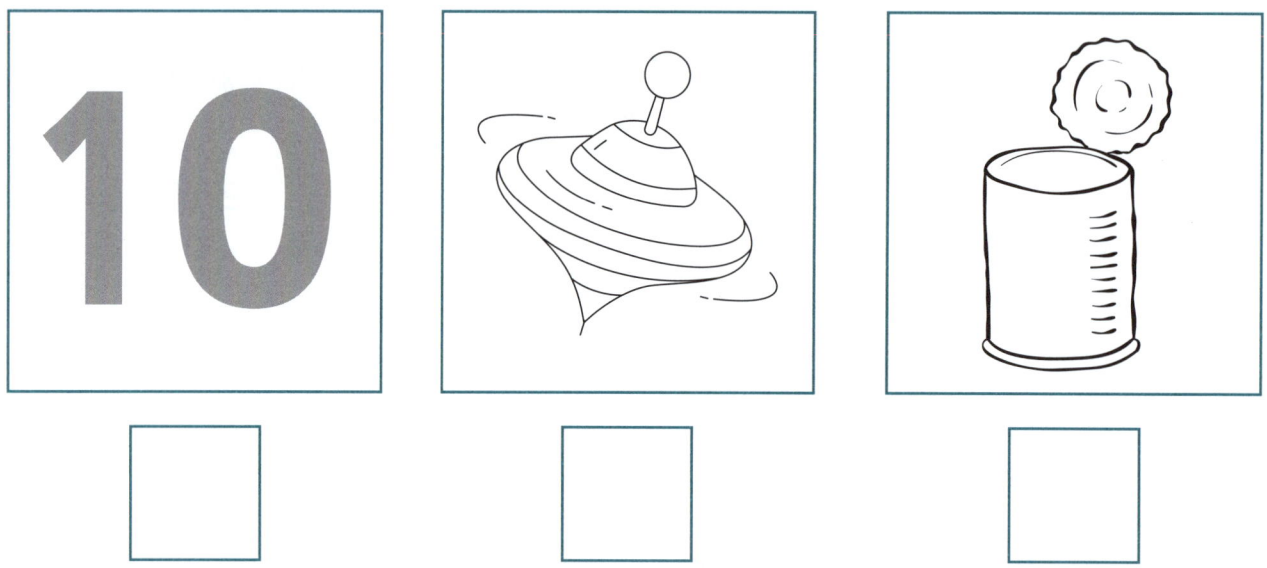

Say the words. Write the letter for the last sound.

t and n

Trace the letter and say the sound.

n n n n n n

Say the words. Circle the letter for the last sound.

Read the black words.
Circle all the coloured words that match the black words.

at   at   as   ta   at   an   sn   at
an   at   an   na   an   an   tn   an

Template 2

Trace the letters and say the sounds.

i i i p p p

Say the words for the pictures.

Join each picture to the letter that matches the first sound in its word.

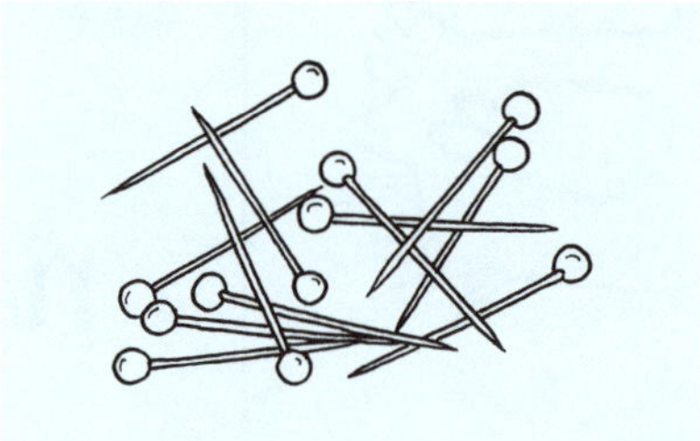

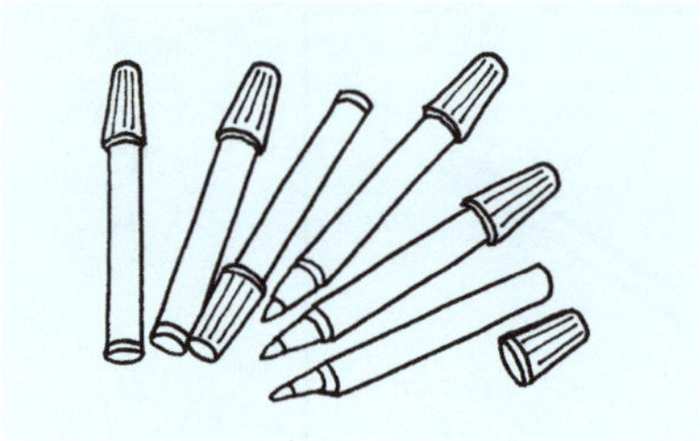

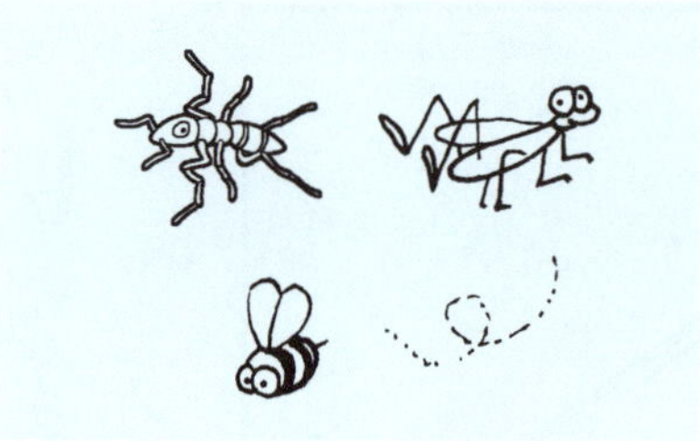

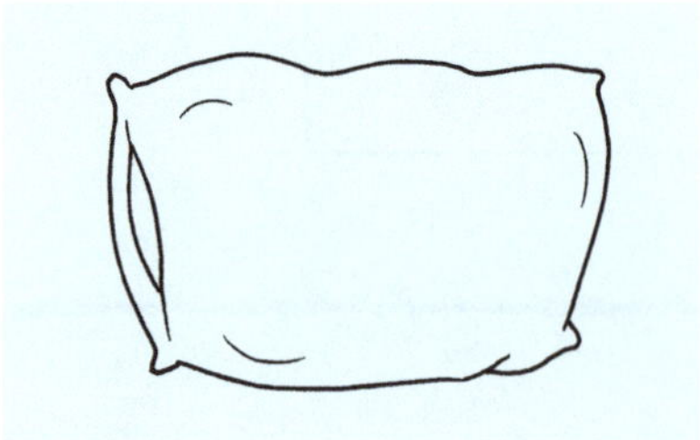

Colour the pictures of things that begin with the sound **p**.

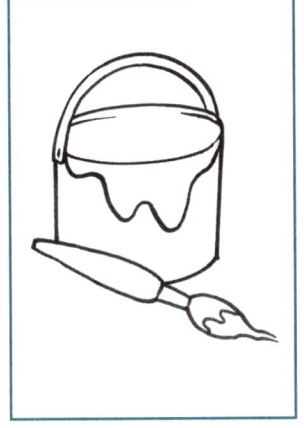   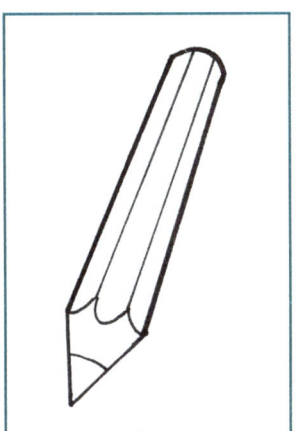

  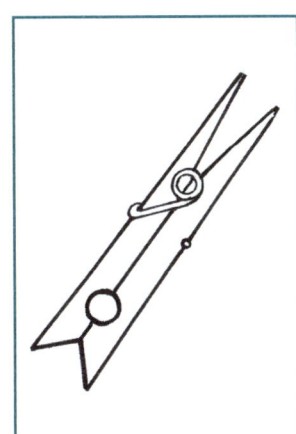 

Read the words.

it   is   in   is   it   in

Read the sentence. Circle **it is in** in the sentence.

It is an ant in a pan.

Trace the words.

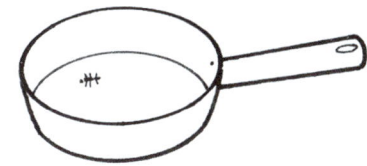

in   in   is   is   it   it

Template 3

> Look back

Check what you know!

Trace the letters and say the letter sounds.

s a t n i p

Write the first letter of each word under each picture.

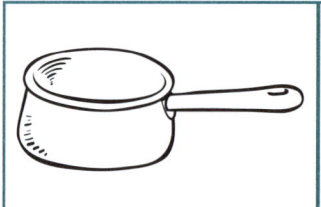  10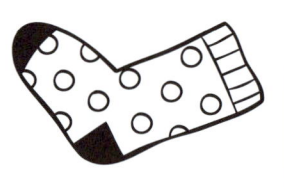

____ an   ____   ____   ____

  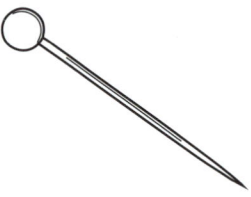 

____   ____   ____ in   ____ it

 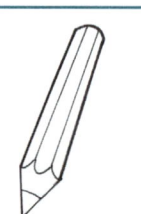  

____   ____   ____   ____

14

Look back

Read and trace the word.

the   the   the

Read the questions. Write ✓ or ✗.

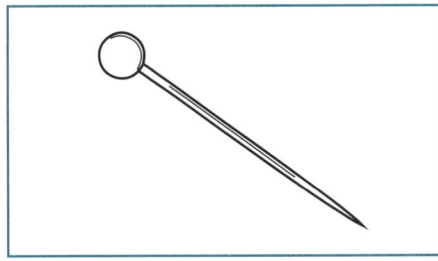 Is it a pin?

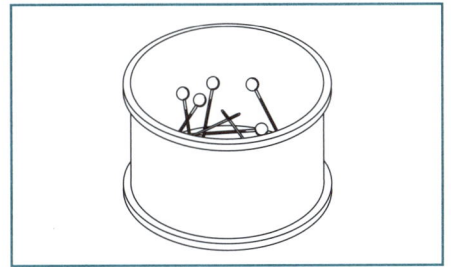 Is a pin in the tin?

 Is the ant in a pan?

Write the word **the** in the box.

15

Template 4

Trace the letters and say the sounds.

o o g g d d

Say the words. Write **o**, **g** or **d** to finish the words.

o, g and d

Trace the letters and say the sounds.

o o g g d d

Say the word. Choose the correct letters to finish the word.

di ____ [d / p]

[s / p] ____ ot

sa ____ [g / d]

t / d ____ a ____ d / n

Read the black words. Circle all the coloured words that match the black words.

| dad | sad | did | dad | dot | dad |

| got | not | got | gap | got | gas |

17

Template 5

Trace the letters and say the sounds.

m m m c c k k

Say the word. Circle the letter for the first sound. Write the word.

k

m

_____

t

c

_____

m

n

_____

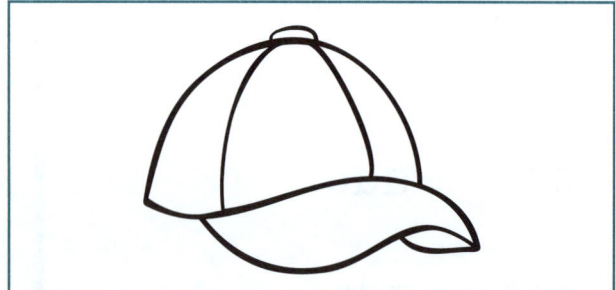

c

m

_____

m, c and k

The robot turns mixed-up letters into words.
Write the words.

1. n c a → 1. can
2. p a m → 2. m____
3. n p a → 3. p____
4. t p o → 4. t____
5. t i k → 5. k____
6. t c o → 6. c____

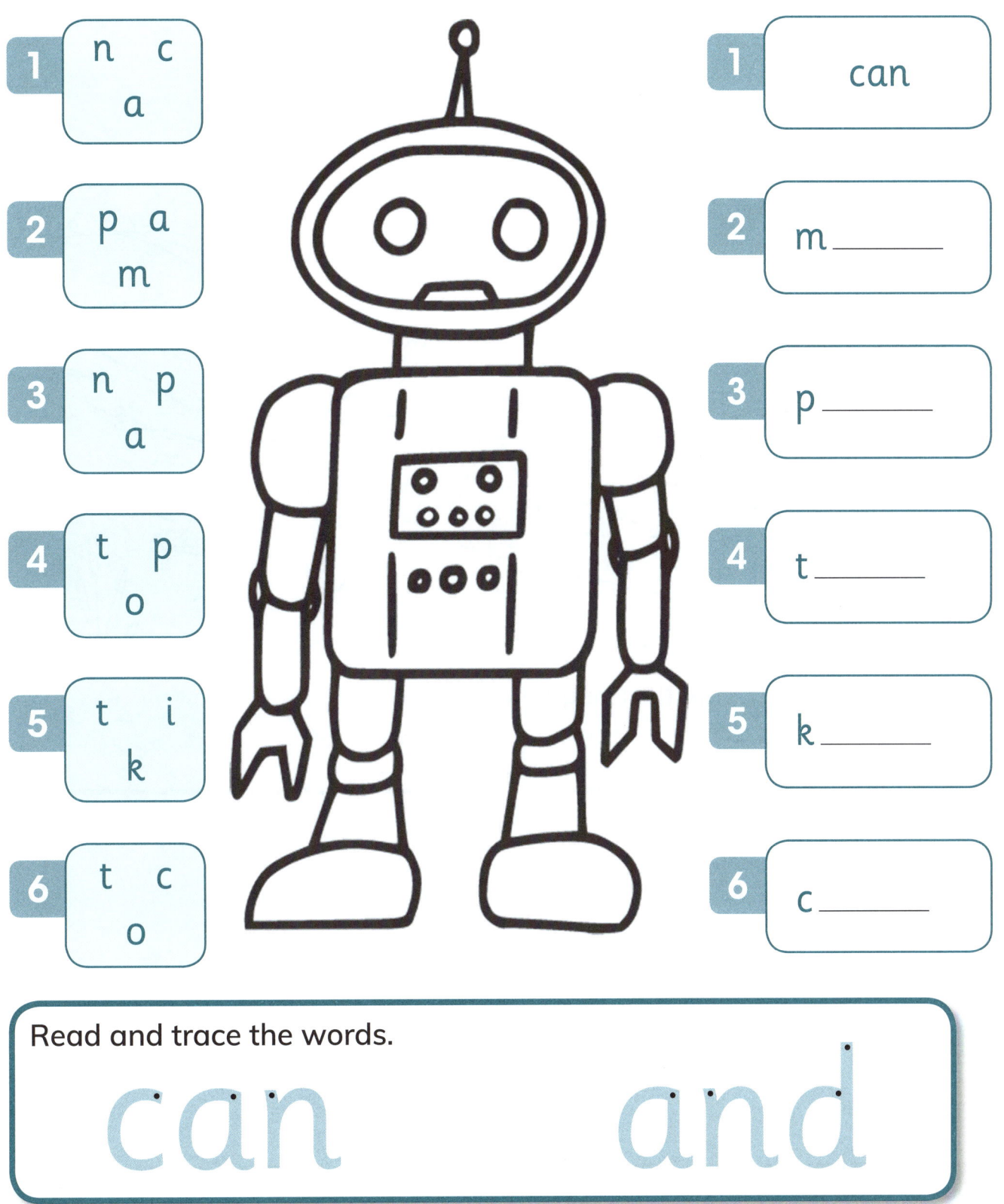

Read and trace the words.

can   and

19

Template 1

Trace the letter and say the sound.

r r r r r r

Circle the things that begin with the sound r.

Draw two more things that begin with r.

Write r next to them.

r, e and u

Trace the letters and say the sounds.

e e e   u u u

Write e or u next to pictures of things with e or u in them.

Colour the e pictures red. Colour the u pictures blue.

Read and trace the words.

get   get

Read the sentence. **Mum, get up!**

up   up

21

Template 6

> Look back

Trace the letters and say the sounds.

c o a d g s e
i k t u r n m p

Write the correct words under the pictures.

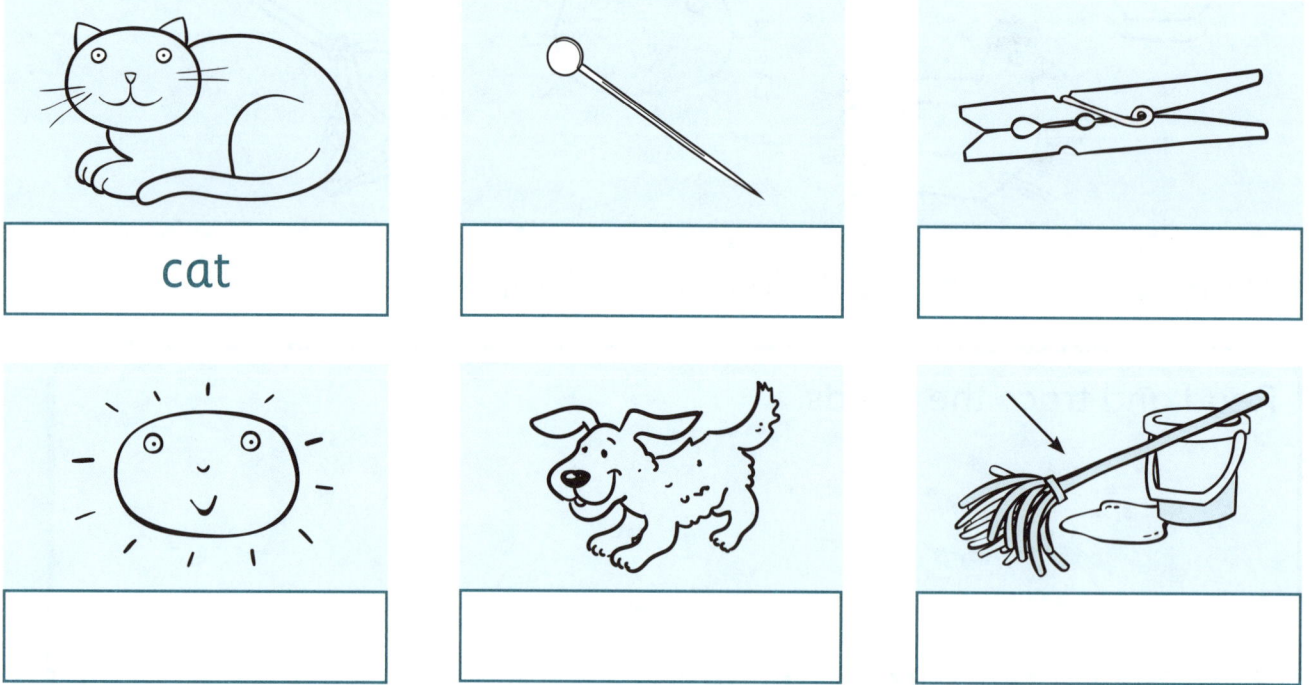

cat

Write two words with **p**.

Write two words with **g**.

Look back

Read and trace the words.

I am   I am

Read the questions. Write ✓ or ✗.

Am I at the top? ☐   Am I ill? ☐

Is the cat sad? ☐   Is the hen red? ☐

Write **I am** in the box.

Template 5

Trace the letters and say the sounds.

h h   b b   l l   f f

The robot turns mixed-up letters into words.
Write the words.

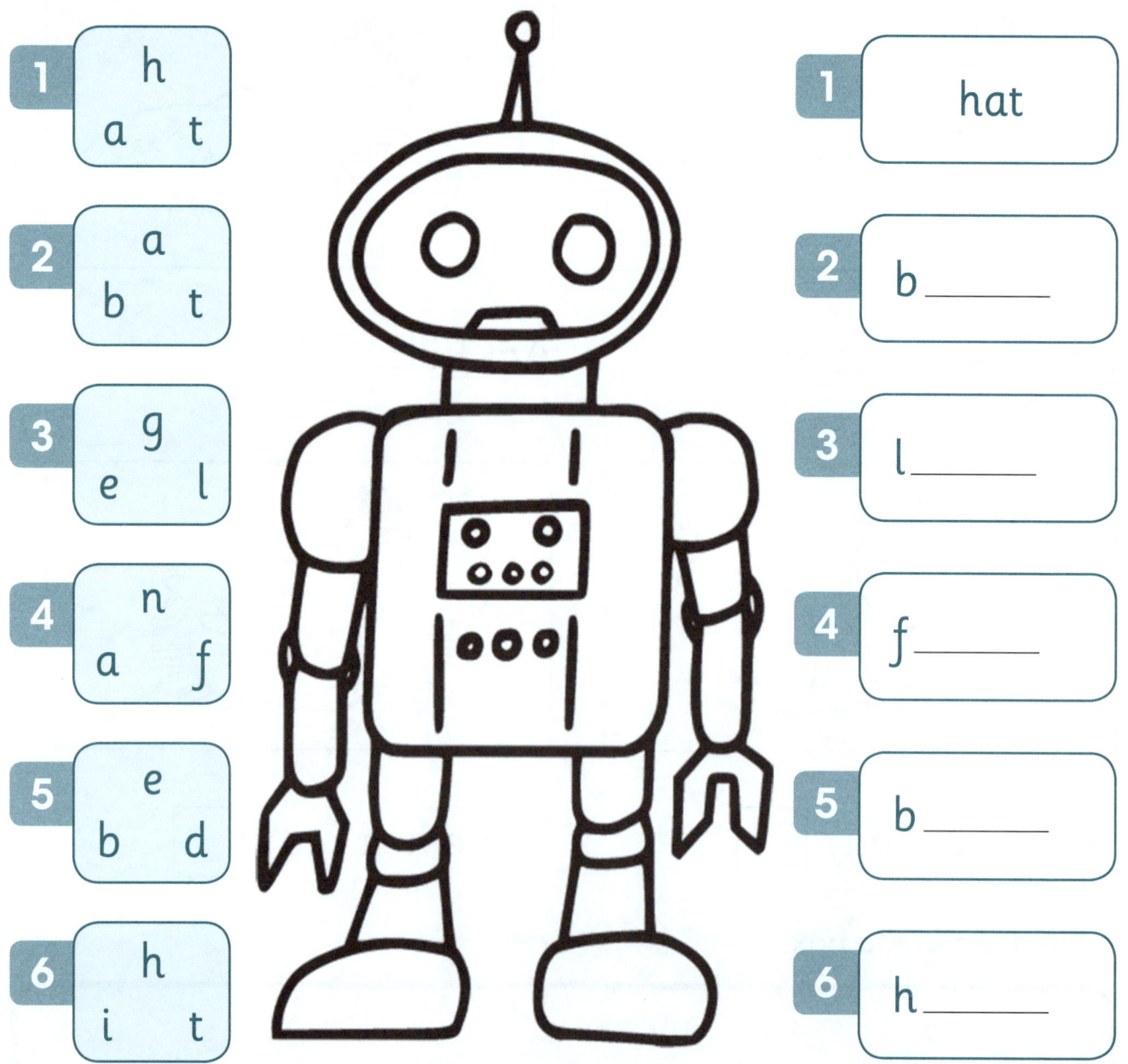

1. h a t
2. a b t
3. g e l
4. n a f
5. e b d
6. h i t

1. hat
2. b _____
3. l _____
4. f _____
5. b _____
6. h _____

24

Read the story.

A man gets on a bus.

The man has a big hat.
Can his hat fit on the bus?

The man is not on the bus …

Draw what happens next.

… but his hat is on the bus!

Read and trace the words

Write the number of times you can see each word in the story.

Template 4

Trace the letters and say the sounds.

ck   ll   ff   ss

Say the words. Write **ck**, **ll**, **ff** or **ss** to finish the words.

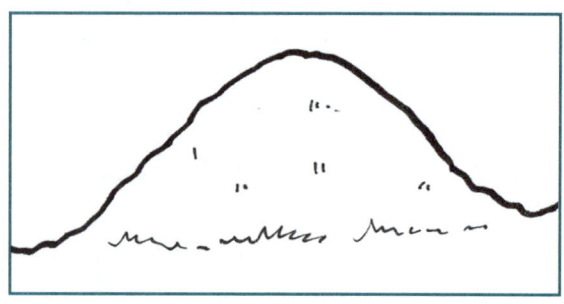

| h | i | |

| o | |

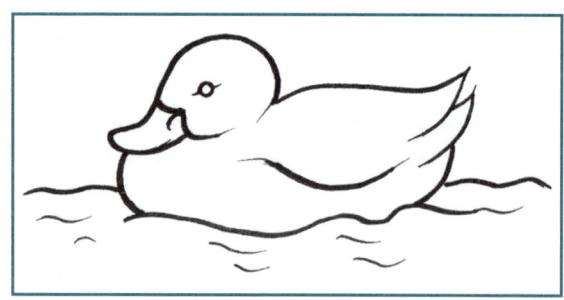

| d | u | |

| m | e | |

Double letters

Trace the letters and say the sounds.

ck ll ff ss

Say the words. Choose the correct letters to finish the words.

 ck / ss

ba _____

 ss / ff

me _____

 ck / ss

chi _____

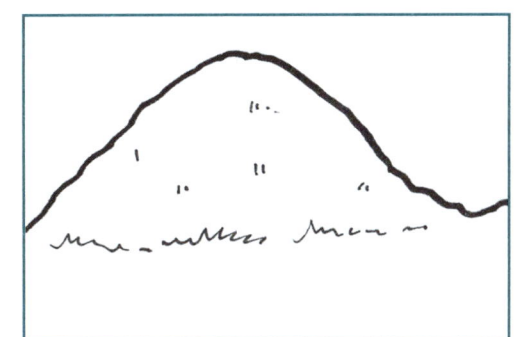 ss / ll

hi _____

Read the black words.
Circle all the coloured words that match the black words.

will   wick   will   well   will   win   will   well

off   of   off   off   of   off   of   off   off   of

27

Template 2

Trace the letters and say the sounds.

j   v   w   x   Say the sounds 'ks' for letter x.

Read and trace the words. Write the correct words under the pictures.

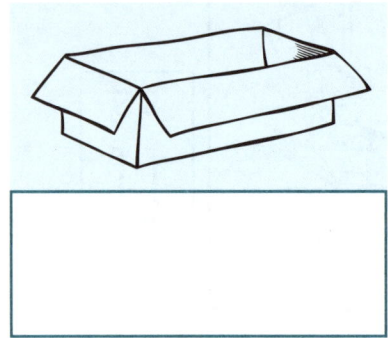

jug
box
vet
web
jog
fox

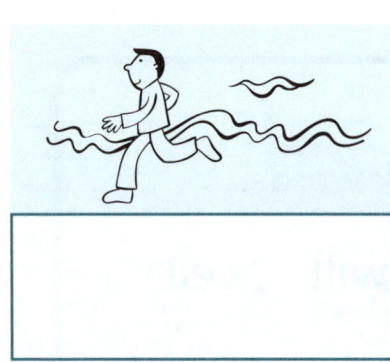

j, v, w and x

Colour the pictures of things that have the sound **w** in them.

 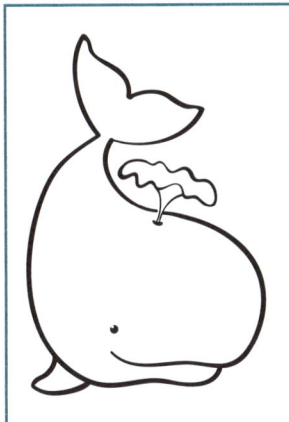  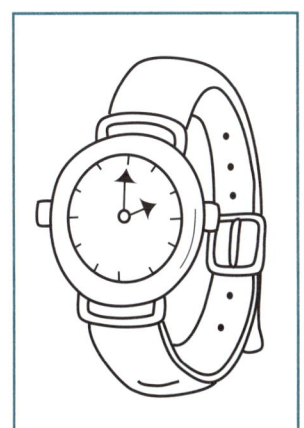

  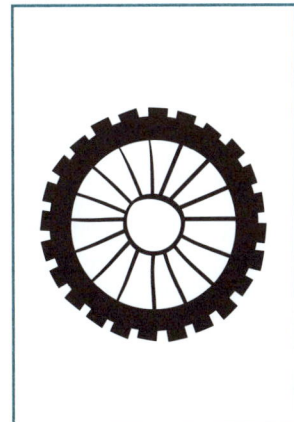 

Read the words.

to   to   of   of

Read the sentence. Find and circle the words in the sentence.

The fox jogs to the box of cats.

Trace the words below.

to   to   of   of

29

Template 2 and 3

Trace the letters and say the sounds.

y z zz qu

Say **z** and **zz** the same way.
Say the sounds '**kw**' for letters **qu**. In these words **q** and **u** appear together.

Say the words for the pictures.

Join each picture to the letter that matches the first sound in its word.

y, z, zz and qu

Read and trace the words.

yes yes no no

Read the questions. Write yes or no.

Is the hen in a box?

_____

Did the duck buzz?

_____

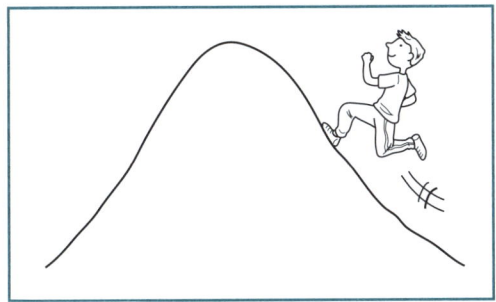

Can I jog to the top of the hill?

_____

Is the zip up?

_____

Template 3

> Look back

Write the letter for the first sound of each word under its picture. Where you see *, write the last letter or letters.

Read and trace the words.

yes yes no no

Read the questions. Write **yes** or **no**.

Is the lid on?

_____

Is a bag in the bed?

_____

Can the cat get in the box?

_____

Can I win?

_____

Template 1

Say the sound for each letter to read the words.

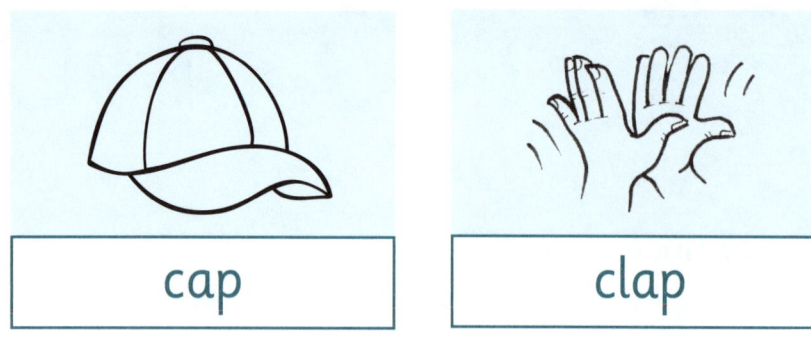

| cap | clap |

Write the correct words under the pictures.

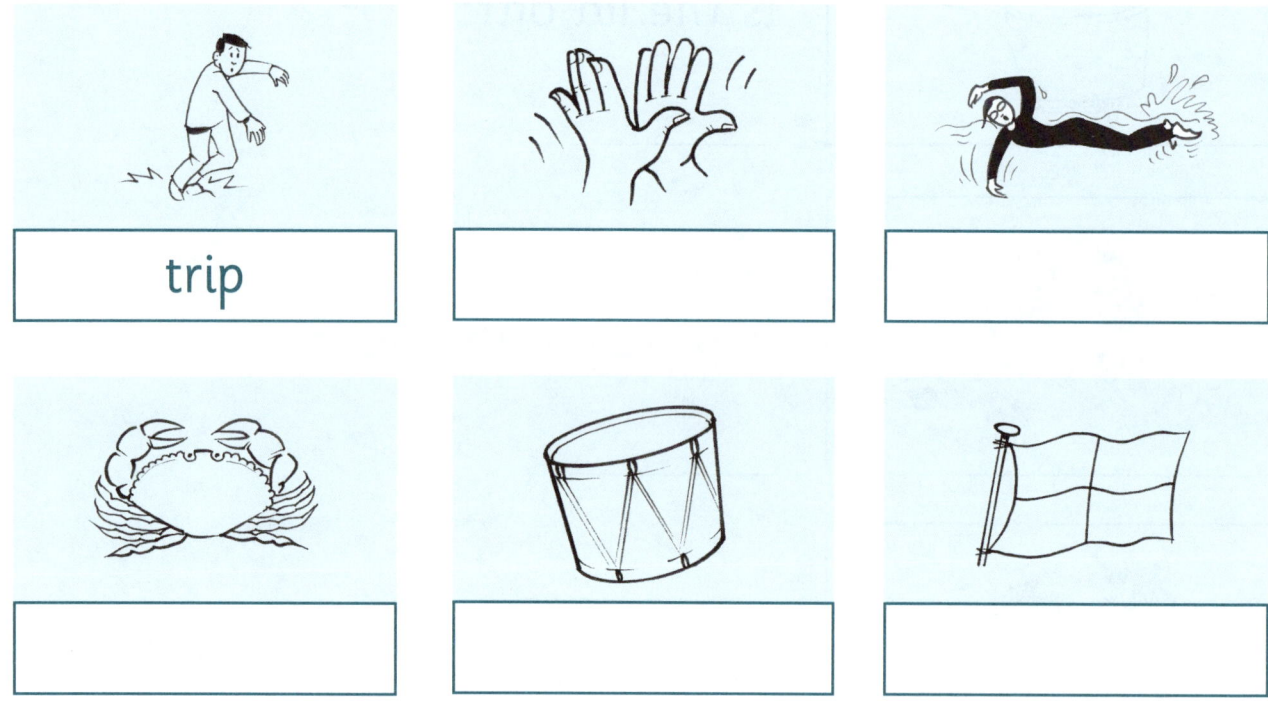

| trip | | |

Finish the words. Draw pictures of the words.

| f | r | |

| s | p | |

Adjacent consonants

Say the sound for each letter to read the word.

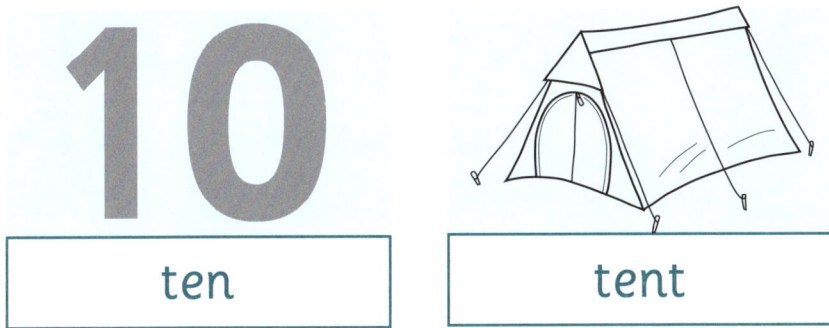

ten

tent

Write the correct words under the pictures.

soft

Finish the words. Draw pictures of the words.

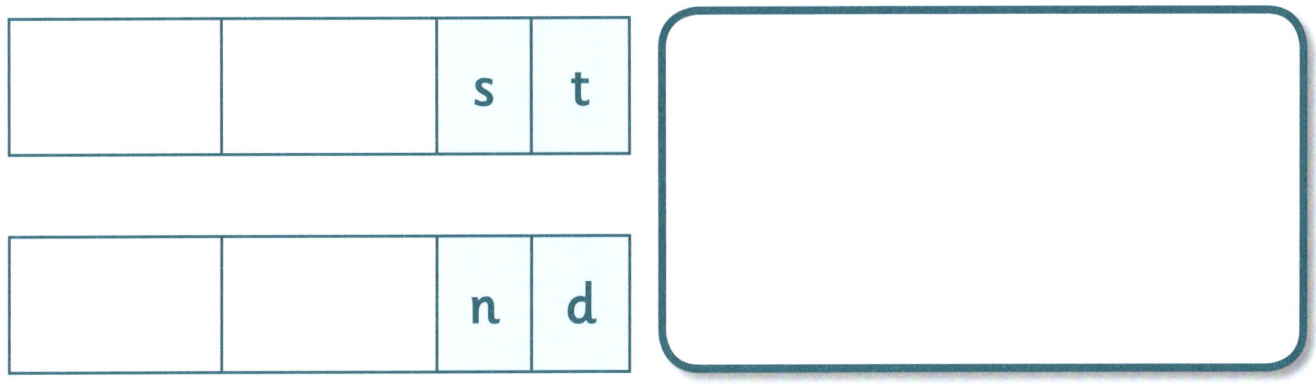

| | | s | t |
| | | n | d |

35

Template 2 and 5

Trace the letters and say the sounds.

ng   ng   nk   nk

Read and trace the words.
Write the correct words under the pictures.

sing

sink

wing

wink

ring

rink

ng, nk and th

Read the story.

This man sits and thinks.

He sings a song.

Then he has a drink.

Draw what happens next.

Then he ...

Read and trace the words.

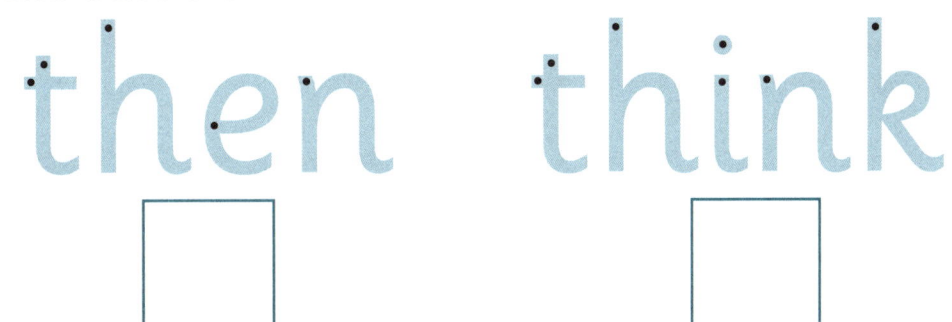

then   think

Write the number of times you can see each word in the story.

Template 1

Trace the letters and say the sounds.

sh sh ch ch

Write **sh** or **ch** next to pictures of things with **sh** or **ch** in them.

Draw another thing that begins with **sh** and **ch**.

Write **sh** or **ch** next to them.

sh and ch

Trace the letters and say the sounds.

sh   sh   ch   ch

Write **sh** or **ch** next to each picture.

Colour the **sh** pictures green. Colour the **ch** pictures purple.

Read and trace the words.

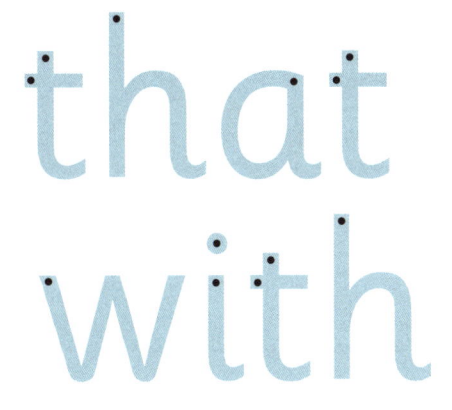

that   that

with   with

Circle **that** and **with** in this sentence.

That is the bag with fish and chips in it.

Template 4

Trace the letters and say the sounds.

ai   ai   ee   ee

Say the words. Write **ai** or **ee** to finish the words.

t _ l

b _

sh _ p

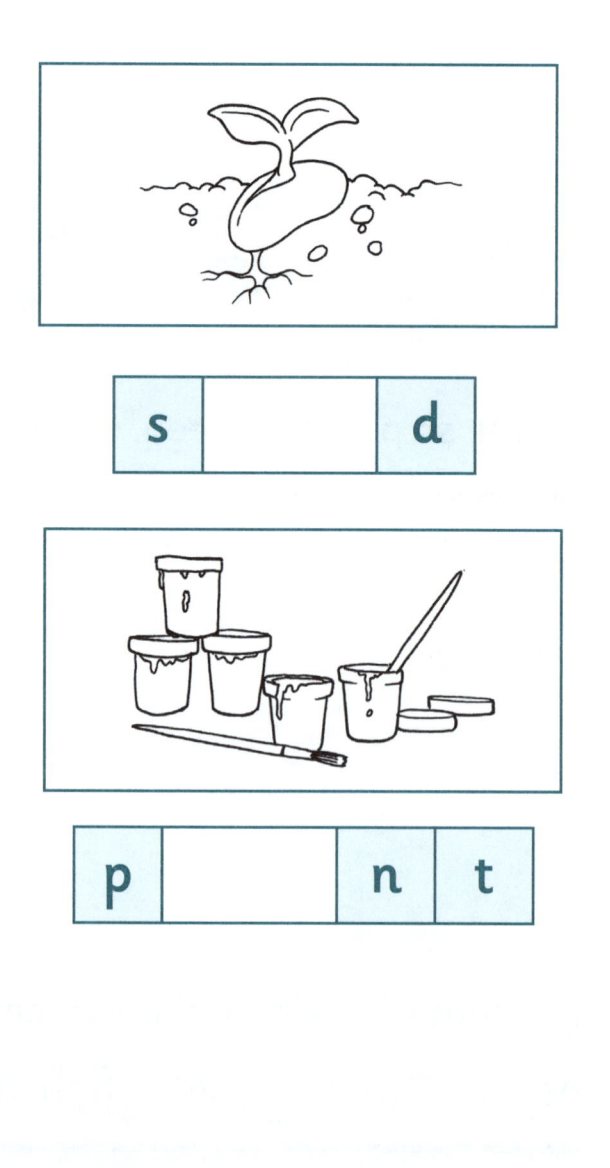

s _ d

p _ n t

ai and ee

Trace the letters and say the sounds.

ai ai ee ee

Say the word. Choose the correct letters to finish the word.

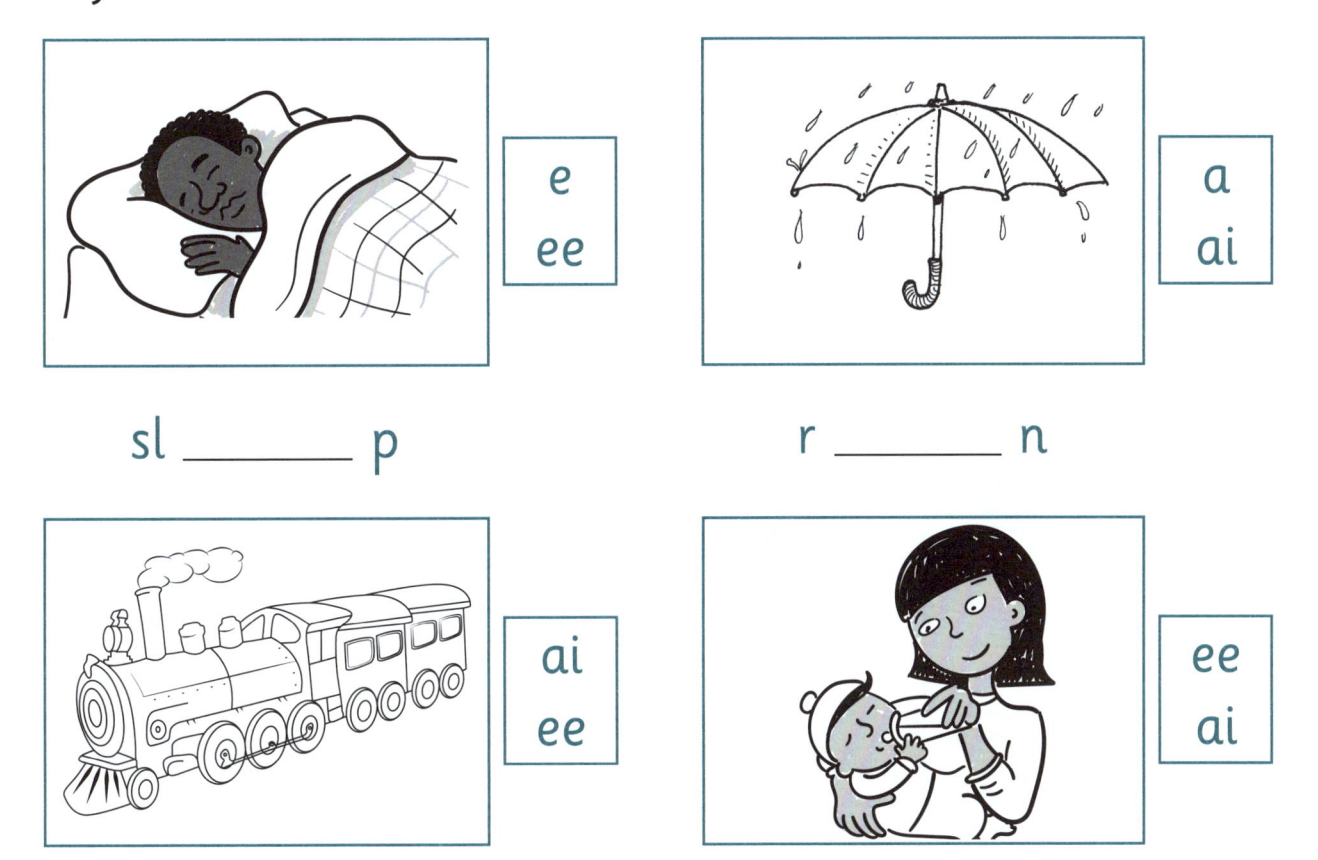

sl _____ p   e / ee

r _____ n   a / ai

tr _____ n   ai / ee

f _____ d   ee / ai

Read the black words.
Circle all the coloured words that match the black words.

they   the   they   that   they   they   the

she   she   he   she   shell   she   she   he

41

Template 6

Trace the letters and say the sounds.

ie ie ie oa oa

Say each word. Write **ie** or **oa** to finish each word.

| g _____ t | t _____ | s _____ p |
| r _____ d | l _____ | g _____ l |

Write the correct words under the pictures.

ie and oa

Read and trace the words.

me   my   go

Write **me**, **my** or **go** to finish the sentences.

Give the pie to _____.

The cat is on _____ bed.

Can I _____ in the boat with Sam?

Write the words **me**, **my** and **go** in the boxes.

43

Template 2, 6

Trace the letters and say the sounds.

Say these as short sounds like **book**.

oo oo   oo oo

Say these as long sounds like **boot**.

Write the correct words under the pictures.

		kangar_____

Write two words with **oo** sounds like **book**.

Write two words with **oo** sounds like **boot**.

oo (long and short)

Say the words. Colour the pictures where oo sounds like oo in wool.

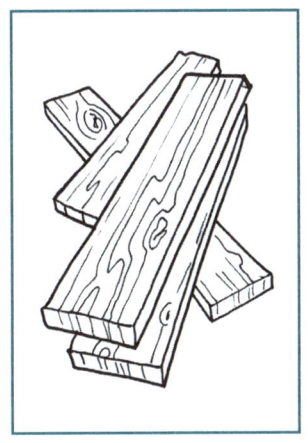

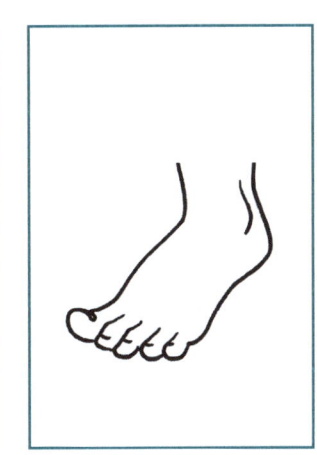

Read the words.

too   look   you

Read the question. Find and circle the words too, look and you.

Can I look at you too?

Trace the words.

too look you

Template 2 and 5

> **Look back**

Check what you know!

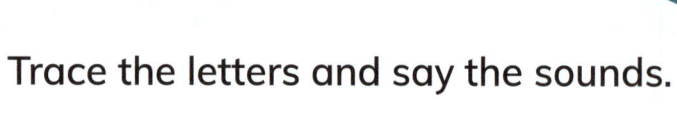

Trace the letters and say the sounds.

ai ee ie oa oo

Read and trace the words. Write the words under the correct picture.

boat
boot 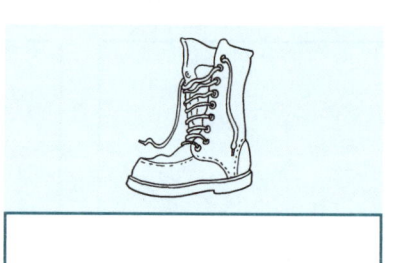 
weed
wood  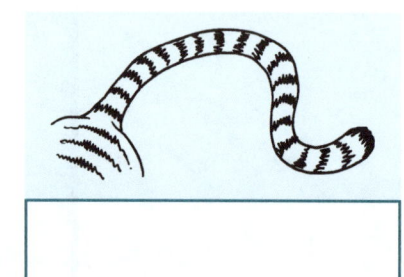
tail
tools

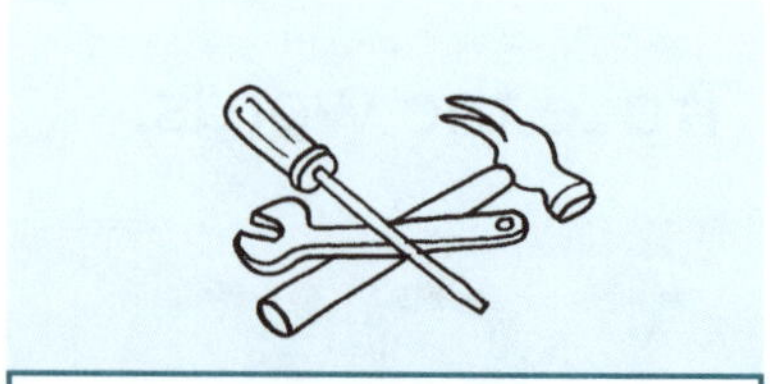

Look back

Read the story.

I can paint with green paint.
Look at my feet!

I will wait for rain.
Then I will need soap.

I will soak this foot.
Next I will soak that foot.

Draw what happens next.

Soon my feet will not
be green.

Trace the letters and say the sounds.

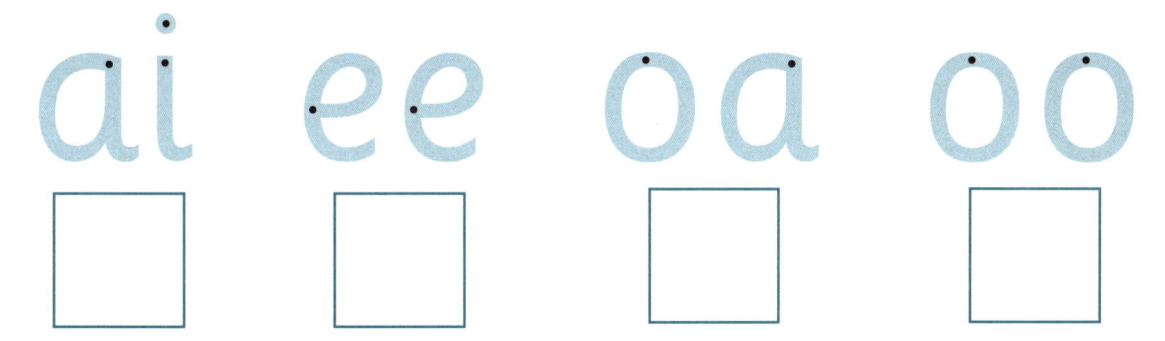

ai ee oa oo

Write the number of times you can see and hear these sounds in words in the story.

Template 4

Trace the letters and say the sounds.

ar   or   ir   er

Say the words. Write **ar**, **or**, **ir** or **er** to finish the words.

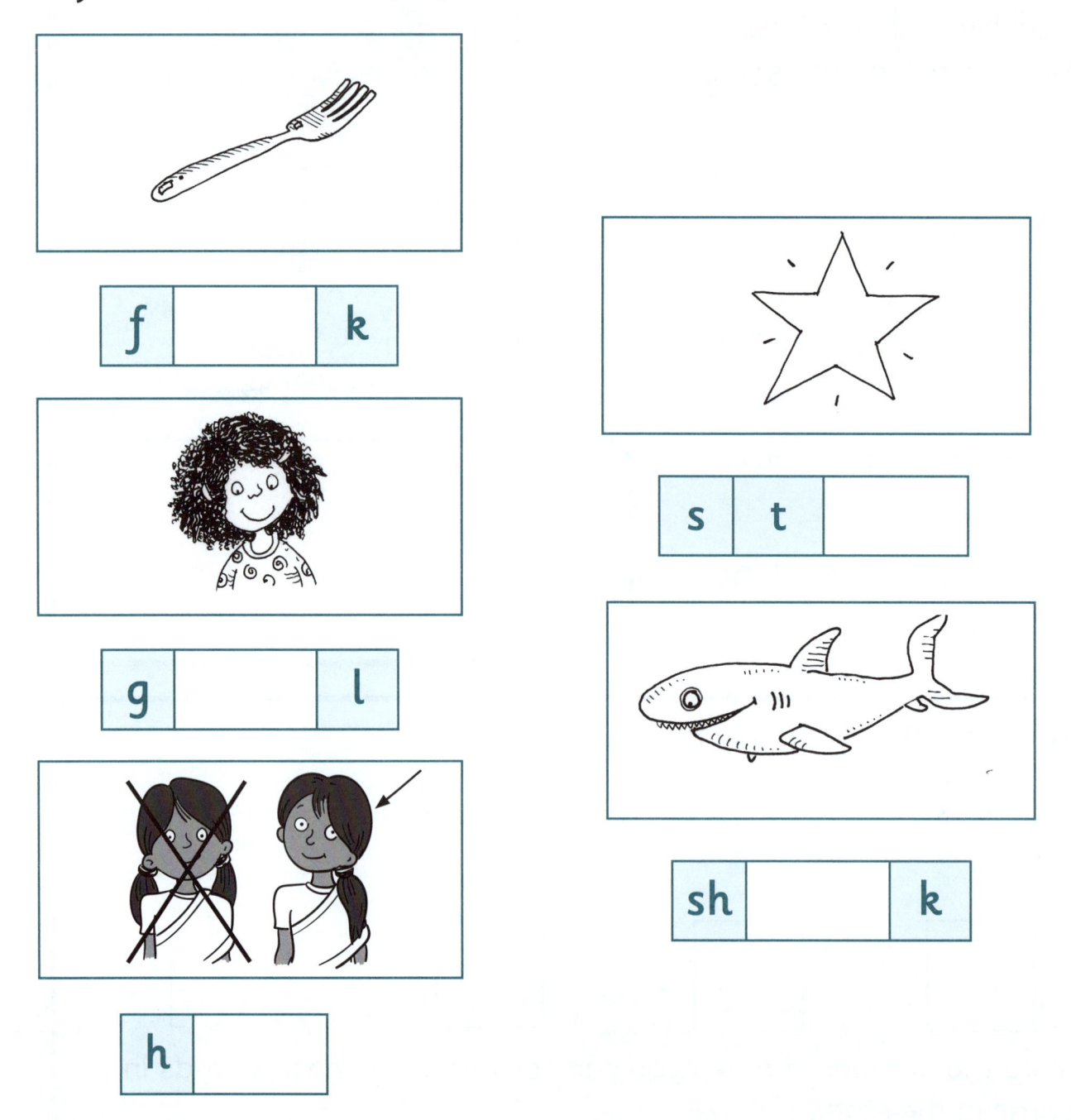

f [ ] k

g [ ] l

h [ ]

s t [ ]

sh [ ] k

ar, or, ir and er

Trace the letters and say the sounds.

ar   or   ir   er

Say the word. Choose the correct letters to finish the word.

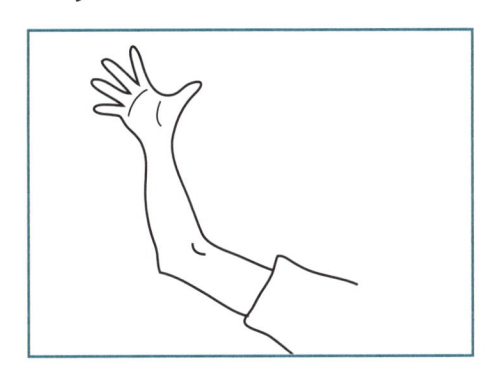

ar / or

_____ m

or / ar

c _____

er / or

m _____ maid

ar / ir

b _____ d

Read the black words.

Circle all the coloured words that match the black words.

are   at   are   are   arc   an   are

for   of   torn   for   tar   for   for

49

Template 5

Trace the letters and say the sounds.

ow   ow   oi   oi

The robot turns mixed-up letters into words. Write the words.

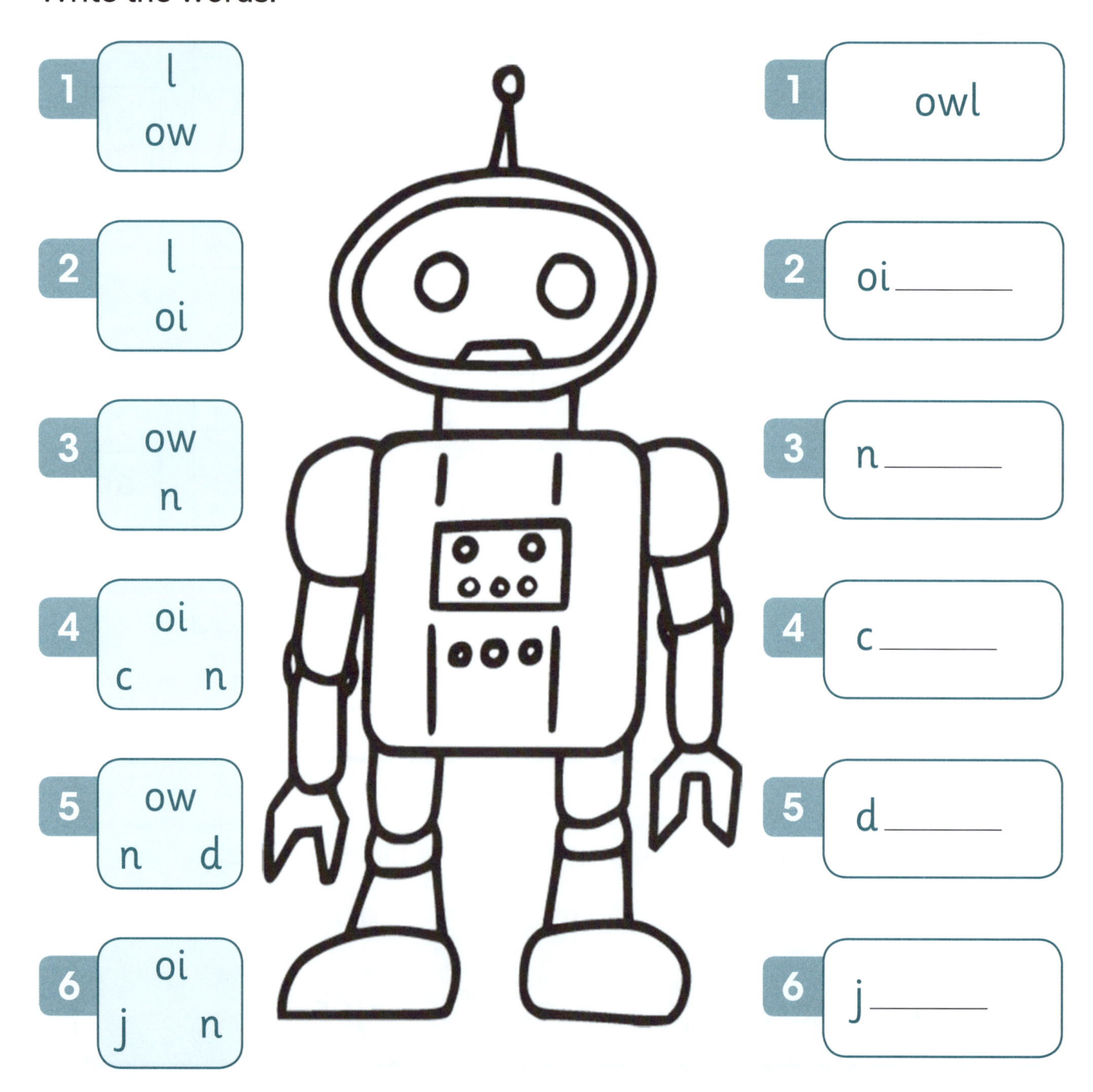

1. l ow
2. l oi
3. ow n
4. oi c n
5. ow n d
6. oi j n

1. owl
2. oi____
3. n____
4. c____
5. d____
6. j____

50

ow and oi

Read the story.

Look at that cow.

She is in the soil.

She is sitting down.

Draw what happens next
Now look at her!

Read and write the words.

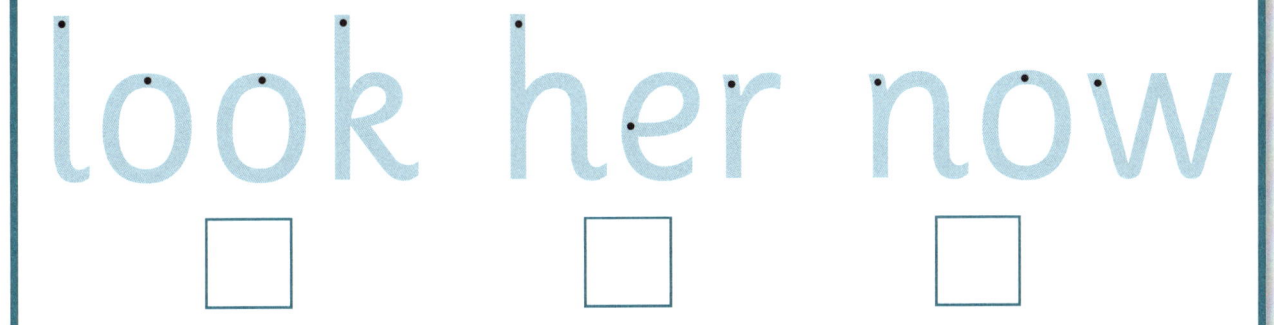

look her now

Write the number of times you can see each word in the story.

51

Template 2

Trace the letters and say the sounds.

ear ear air air

Read and trace the words. Write the words under the pictures.

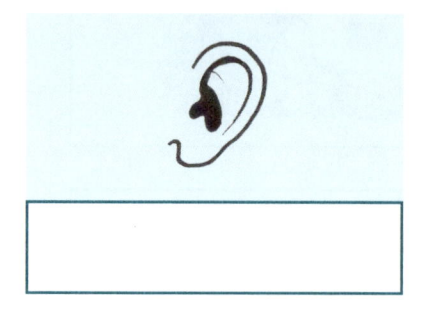

ear

air

hear

hair

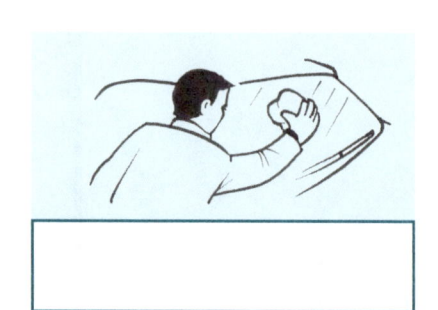

clear

chair

ear and air

Colour the pictures of things that have the sound **air** in them.

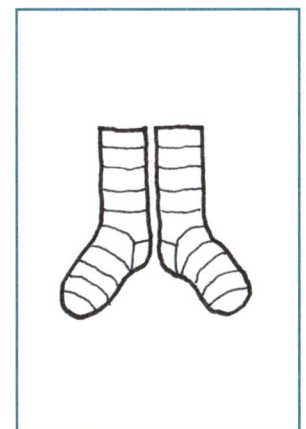

Read the word.

was   was

Read the sentence.

Find and circle the word in the sentence.

Her hair was long and fair.

Trace the words.

was   was

Template 3

> Look back

Check what you know!

Write the words.

Use these letters: sh ch th ng nk

ship	chick	moth	ring

chin	sheep	fish

Write the words.

Use these letters: ie ai oo oa ea oi ow ar or air

tail	fork	pie	coat

spoon	book	car	tear

cow	pizza	chair

54

Look back

Read and trace the words.

yes yes no no

Read the questions. Write yes or no.

Can you hang a coat on a hook?
_____

Is this a shark with sharp teeth?
_____

Is the cow in the river?
_____

Can a fish sit on a chair?
_____

Phonics Workbook A

> Teaching phonics using Phonics Workbook A

Cambridge Primary English Phonics Workbooks A and B provide a structured introduction to phonics to underpin the Cambridge Primary English course. The books can also supplement other English courses.

Phonics is an important skill to learn in the early stages of reading and writing. This book is intended to be used with children who are just beginning to learn phonics. They are likely to be aged between 4 and 5 when they use Phonics Workbook A, while Phonics Workbook B is intended to form part of the Stage 1. The books are appropriate for learners who have English as a first or as a second language. If you are working with children for whom English is a second language, make sure that the vocabulary used in the book is familiar to them. You may also need to support bilingual learners with their pronunciation of letter sounds.

Phonics Workbook A introduces learners to one way of reading and representing each of the 44 sounds in the English language. The letter patterns (graphemes) chosen to represent each of the sounds (phonemes) are those most commonly used in reading books available for learners at this stage.

What is phonics?

'Phonics' is the name that we use to describe the relationship between the spoken sounds and the written letters in a language. So, when we teach learners 'phonics', we are teaching them to match a written letter, or letters, with a spoken sound and to use this knowledge to read and spell.

The earliest stages of phonics

Before learners are taught to link letters to sounds, they need to learn to listen for sounds in words. For very young learners, this can be difficult and they are likely to find it easier to hear bigger 'chunks' of language before they can discriminate the individual sounds in words. So, you could do these things.

- Teach them to count the number of words in a short phrase or sentence. Give them some counters and ask them to push forward one counter for each word you say. For example, **the black cat** = three counters.

- Teach them to clap the number of syllables in longer words, such as in their names, in classroom objects and in familiar animals. For example, **cro-co-dile** = three claps.

- Teach them to play with rhymes. Sing and say common rhymes; if you omit the rhyming word each time, can the learners provide it?

- Teach them to make a silly string of rhyming syllables, such as cat–lat–pat–wat.

Saying the sounds in words

When you talk about sounds in words, use the sound linked to the letter, not its name. For example, for the letter **k** say k^{uh} instead of **kay** and for the letter **b** say b^{uh} instead of **bee**. When you say consonants, try to say as little vowel sound around the consonant as possible. For example, say **fff** instead of **fuh**. Here are some ways to practise this.

- Teach learners to listen for the first sound in a word. Play games like 'I spy with my little eye …'.

- Put toys on the table and ask learners to find which ones share the same first sound. For example, say: *Find another toy with the same first sound as 'tiger'*.

- Once learners can confidently hear the first sound in a word, ask them to listen while you say all the sounds in a word and see if they can tell you what the word is. Put objects or pictures on the table and say the sounds in a three-letter word (for example, **c-a-t** or **l-o-g**) and ask the learners to identify the word. Puppets are very useful for this type of activity – make sure that learners know the puppet can only speak in sounds, not words.

Teaching using Phonics Workbook A

- When learners can clearly hear the sounds in a word, ask them to say all of the sounds so that you or another child can try to find the matching picture. Let the learners use puppets for this activity too.

- Teach learners to use 'phonic fingers' to show the sounds in a word. They should hold up one finger to represent each sound, and then sweep the index finger of their other hand across all of the fingers that are held up and say the whole word.

  For example:

  c-a-t   cat

  Ideally, learners should be confident at hearing the sounds in a word before they begin to use this workbook.

- Using common words, show them how sometimes blending is trickier or not as helpful. For example, **the**, **me**, **would**.

Using this workbook

Introducing the sounds

The activities in Phonics Workbook A are intended to follow an introductory session, which you do with the learners using objects, pictures and cards showing letters and letter patterns that they can manipulate. You will find it useful to have sets of cards showing all the letters (graphemes): single as in **m**, double as in **ch** and triple as in **air**. As new graphemes for sounds are introduced, make cards for them too.

Before you introduce each activity, spend time exploring a sound orally while showing the learners letters. Phonics is best presented as a multisensory activity to support learners to remember letter formation, letter names and associated sounds. Activities you could use include the following.

- Making sets of objects or pictures that begin with the target sound and asking learners to say each word aloud, to say just the first sound and then to place the letter card next to each object or picture. Then introduce a few more examples and ask the learners to decide whether or not they belong to the same set.

- Making opportunities for learners to make letters out of playdough or clay, or to write them in sand, salt or shaving foam with their fingers before they try to write the letters in the book.

- Helping learners to create new words by combining known letters. This allows them to reinforce their understanding of the sounds in words and the sounds represented by each of the new letters or letter patterns.

Introducing the activity pages

In Phonics Workbook A, there are six different activity page templates. (Note there is some variation within the templates.)

Activities include:

- tracing and writing the letter shape
- saying and hearing the sounds in words
- reading words containing the sound
- saying and writing short words.

The workbook is cumulative: once letters and sounds have been introduced, they are practised and used on subsequent pages. If the learners appear to have 'forgotten' what was previously taught, revisit the earlier pages and additional activities in order to secure and consolidate the knowledge.

Writing the letters

As part of learning to recognise a letter and its sound, it is important that learners learn to 'feel' its shape by writing it. Most of the activities in this workbook include opportunities for writing and tracing letters, but you should also offer additional experiences so that learners automatically write the letter correctly. It is important to be consistent in letter formation.

Reading and writing

The activities on pages 8 to 31 introduce all the letters of the alphabet. Once learners are familiar with these letter sounds, encourage them to use

Phonics Workbook A

them as the basic building blocks when reading and writing. Pages 36 to 53 introduce the trickier letter sounds when one sound is represented by two or more letters, for example the sound at the beginning of **sh**op or the vowel sound in r**ai**n or r**igh**t.

When reading, encourage learners to **blend** sounds together in order to read and say the word – for example, **t-r-ai-n train**.

By the time learners have finished this workbook, they will know at least one way of representing all the sounds they need to write in English. Encourage them to say the word they want to write, then to segment it into the individual sounds – for example, **clown c-l-ow-n**.

Common words

Most sessions end with the introduction of associated common words. These words need to be learned because parts of them do not follow phonic rules. Encourage the learners to try a 'phonics first' approach to tackling these words for reading and spelling. They should apply what they know and try to work out the word. As they do so, they will begin to see where they need to tweak certain letters or sounds.

Assessment

This workbook is cumulative, allowing learners to practise what they have previously learned. Use observations of their progress to identify when they are struggling and, if necessary, revise activities, both in the workbook and using your own resources.

In addition, there are Look back pages at the end of every section. Use these to assess and monitor learning. Before you progress beyond a Look back page, make sure that learners can read all of the short texts and read and write all of the words.

Teaching using Phonics Workbook A

Teaching using template 1

Template 1 is used as follows:

Page numbers	Phonics focus	Words to look out for
4–5	Rhyming words	bat, hat, cat, mat, pat man–pan, peg–leg, pin–chin, sun–run, box–fox
8–9	**s** and **a**	sun, sea, swim, swimming, sandcastle, sand, sandals, socks, star, spade, sit
20–21	**r**, **e** and **u**	roof, rhino, run, rat, rabbit, race, road, river
34–35	Adjacent consonants	trip, clap, swim, crab, drum, flag, soft, help, desk, tent, jump, milk
38–39	**sh** and **ch**	lunchbox, sandwich, chest, chick, shark, shell, fish, dish, brush, chair

Teaching sequence

1 On most pages following this template, you will start by saying the sound aloud and asking the learners to repeat it with you. Please note that this panel is not present on page 4.

2 Ask the learners to use their fingers to draw the letter in the air, on a table, and on the back of their other hand. Each time they draw the letter shape, ask them to say its sound. The learners can then trace the letter inside the outlines on the page in the workbook while you watch to ensure correct letter formation. As the learners write each letter, they should say the sound.

3 Read the instruction aloud to the learners. This is primarily a listening activity, not a writing activity. Together, search for words that match the pattern given. Learners may identify words in addition to those shown above, or they may not find them all. Once you have identified words together, allow the learners to circle or label them as requested in the instruction.

4 Read the next instruction aloud to the learners. Before they start to draw, ask them to suggest a list of words that might be appropriate. All the learners should draw their pictures in their workbook and write the sounds.

5 If a new letter is introduced, repeat the sequence of drawing this letter as outlined in Step 2 earlier. If it is the same letter as before, watch while the learners write it to promote good letter formation.

6 Read the instruction aloud to the learners. Ask them to name all of the pictures. Once they know the words, ask the learners to decide whether or not they feature the sound they are working on. If the words do feature the sound, learners should write the letter next to the picture and colour in the picture as suggested in the instruction. Learners can cross out pictures that should not be included.

7 This panel is used to introduce common, sometimes tricky words that cannot be read using phonics alone. Read the word aloud for the learners. Each time they finish writing the word over the letters shown, ask them to say the word aloud.

8 Read the sentence aloud to the learners. Ask them to follow with their fingers, pointing to each word as you read it aloud. Remind the learners of the target word. Ask them to re-read the sentence with you, pointing to each word as they do so. Finally, ask the learners to re-read the sentence themselves, ringing the target words when they see them.

59

Phonics Workbook A

Teaching using template 2

Template 2 is used as follows:

Page numbers	Phonics focus	Words to look out for
6–7	Words that start with the same letter sound	tent, towel, table, tooth, toes, toys
12–13	i and p	paint, pocket, picture, pencil, peg, puppet
28–29	j, v, w and x	web, whale, watch, win, wheel
30	y, z, zz and qu	yawn, yoghurt, quiet, queen, zoo, zebra
36	ng, nk	sing, sink, wing, wink, ring, rink
46	Look back	n/a
52–53	ear, air	hair, funfair, pair, stairs, chair, airport

In some instances, one page of this template has been used with another page from a different template.

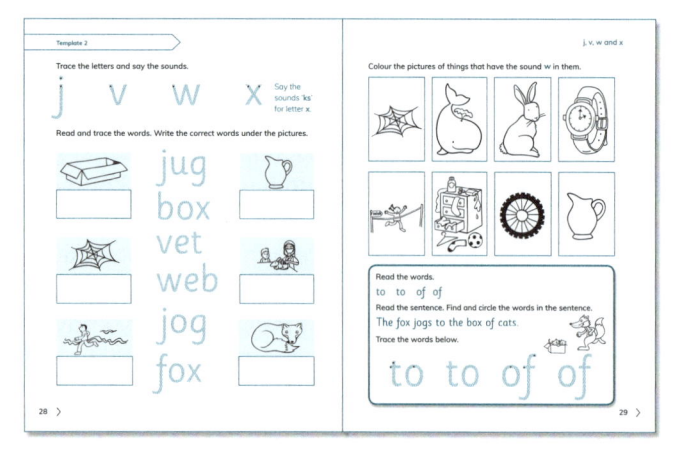

Teaching sequence

1. On most pages following this template, you will start by saying the sound aloud and asking the learners to repeat it with you. This first panel is not included on page 6.
2. Ask the learners to use their fingers to draw the letter in the air, on a table, and on the back of their other hand. Each time they draw the letter shape, ask them to say its sound. The learners can then trace the letter inside the outlines on the page in the workbook, while you watch to ensure correct letter formation. As they write each letter, they should say the sound.
3. Again, this panel is not present on page 6. Read the instruction to the learners. Challenge them to use what they know to say the letters sounds or to sound out the words in the central column. Check that the vocabulary is familiar. Once the learners know the words, they should trace over them.
4. Identify the pictures. Make sure that the learners are familiar with the words. Once they have joined each sound or word to its picture, ask them to sound out and copy the word in the box under each picture. Please note that this stage is not included on page 12.
5. Read the instruction aloud to the learners. Together, name all of the pictures. Ask them to identify which pictures match the instruction. Let them colour or circle the pictures as instructed.
6. This panel is used to introduce common, sometimes tricky words that cannot be read using phonics alone. Read the word aloud for the learners. Each time they finish writing the words over the letters shown, ask them to say the word aloud. Please note that this panel is not included on page 7.
7. Read the sentence aloud to the learners. Ask them to follow with their fingers, pointing to each word as you read it aloud. Remind the learners of the target word or words. Ask them to re-read the sentence with you, pointing to each word as they do so. Finally, ask the learners to re-read the sentence themselves, circling the target words when they see them and, where instructed, trace the letters or words too.

Teaching using Phonics Workbook A

Teaching using template 3

Template 3 is used as follows:

Page numbers	Phonics focus	Words to look out for
14–15	Look back	Note: initial letters only requested for other pictures: **p, t, t, s, a, n, p, s, s, p, a, t**
31	y, z, zz and qu	zip, buzz, no, yes
32–33	Look back	apple, banana, cat, duck, egg, fish, goat, hat, insect, jug, kangaroo, lion, man, nose, orange, penguin, quack, rabbit, sun, tiger, umbrella, van, web, box, yawn, zebra, sock, doll
54–55	Look back	ship, chick, moth, ring, wink, sheep, fish, tail, pie, coat, spoon, book, car, fork, cow, coin, chair, tear

Please note that template 3 is used mainly for Look back and assessment.

Teaching sequence

1. Note: this panel is only present on page 14. Say the sound aloud and ask the learners to repeat it with you. Check that they know the sounds. The learners can then trace the letter inside the outlines on the page in the workbook, while you watch to ensure correct letter formation. As they write each letter, they should say the sound.
2. This instruction is slightly different on the different pages, as the learners become increasingly able to write more independently. Read the instruction aloud to them. Ask them to identify all of the pictures on the sheet. Agree what should be written in the space underneath each picture. Allow them to work independently to complete the page.

   Assess their learning and progress, and identify any sounds of which they are unsure.
3. This panel is used to introduce common, sometimes tricky words that cannot be read using phonics alone. Read the word aloud for the learners. Ask them to trace the words. Each time they finish writing the word over the letters shown, ask the learners to say the word aloud.
4. Read the instruction aloud to the learners. Ask them to look at each of the pictures, then to read each question aloud. The questions refer to the pictures. On page 15, the learners should indicate 'yes' with a tick ✓ and 'no' with a cross ✗, but on pages 31, 33 and 55, they should write 'yes' or 'no' to answer the questions. When learners have correctly completed pages 32 and 54, these pages can make useful tabletop charts to remind them of the letters and sounds they may need while they are writing.

Phonics Workbook A

Teaching using template 4

Template 4 is used as follows:

Page numbers	Phonics focus	Words to look out for
10–11	**t** and **n**	ten, top, hat, sat, hen, tin, pin, net
16–17	**o**, **g** and **d**	dig, pot, log, dot, dog; dip, pot, sad, dad
26–27	Double letters: **ck**, **ll**, **ff**, **ss**	hill, off, duck, mess, back, mess, chick, hill
40–41	**ai**, **ee**	tail, seed, bee, paint, sheep, sleep, rain, train, feed
42–43	**ie**, **oa**	goat, tie, soap, road, lie, goal, boat, pie, coat
48–49	**ar**, **or**, **ir** and **er**	fork, star, girl, shark, her, arm, car, mermaid, bird

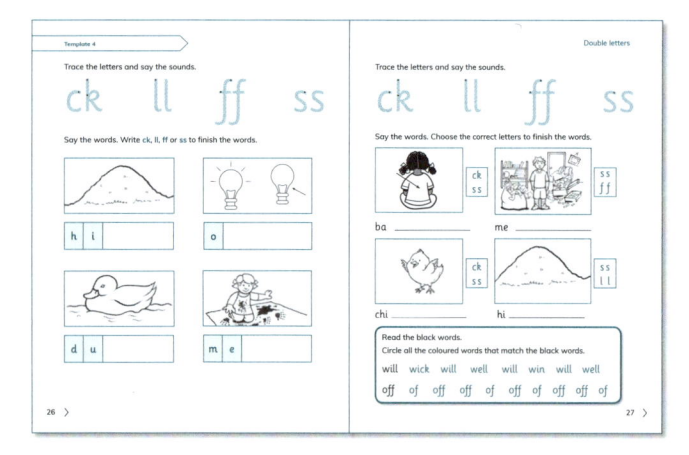

Teaching sequence

1 Say the sound aloud and ask the learners to repeat it with you. Although the combinations of letters may be new, the letters themselves should be familiar. Learners should then trace the letter inside the outlines on the page in the workbook, while you watch to ensure correct letter formation.

2 Read the instruction aloud to the learners. It is slightly different on page 10. Ask the learners to identify the pictures. They should then use 'phonic fingers' (see pages 56–57) to show how many sounds there are in each word. There is the same number of boxes as there are sounds in each word. Ask the learners to identify the missing sound, then the missing letter(s) in each word. Point out that they can write two or more letters in longer boxes if the two or more letters represent just one sound. Leave them to complete the page independently. Make sure learners then blend the sounds to read the words to check their spellings are correct.

3 Ask the learners to identify the sound made by each of the letters. They should be able to trace and write the letters with good letter formation.

4 Read the instruction aloud to the learners. Ask them to identify the pictures. Explain that they have to write letters to finish the words. Show them the boxes and tell them that they must choose from one of the two choices provided in the box. Model completing the first box together, then leave them to finish the task independently. Make sure learners then blend the sounds to read the words to check their spellings are correct.

5 This panel is used to introduce common, sometimes tricky words that cannot be read using phonics alone. Read the instruction aloud to the learners. Identify the words in the box. Explain that they need to look carefully at the target word and then find it in the line. Warn them that there are some tricks on the page, so they will have to look very carefully.

Teaching using Phonics Workbook A

Teaching using template 5

Template 5 is used as follows:

Page numbers	Phonics focus	Words to look out for
18–19	**m, c** and **k**	kit, cat, man, cap, can, map, pan, top, cot
24–25	**h, b, l** and **f**	hat, bat, leg, fan, bed, hit
37	**ng, nk** and **th**	n/a
47	Look back	n/a
50–51	**ow** and **oi**	owl, oil, now, coin, down, join

In some instances, one page of this template has been used with another page from a different template.

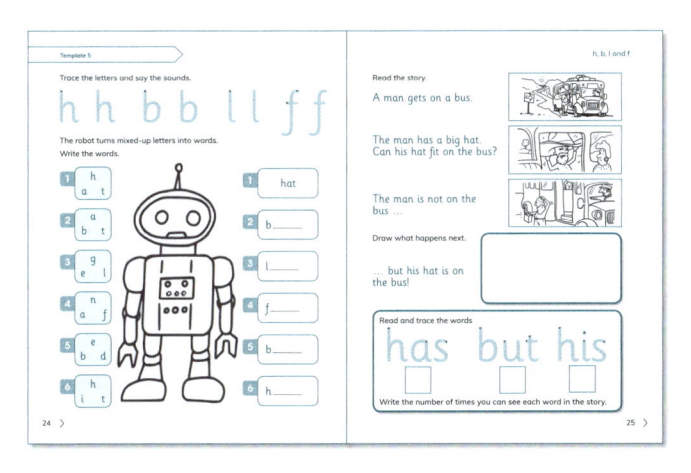

Teaching sequence

1. Where there is a panel at the top of the page, say the sounds aloud and ask the learners to repeat them with you. Ask them to use their fingers to draw each letter in the air, on a table, and on the back of their other hand. Each time they draw the letter shape, ask them to say its sound. The learners can then trace the letters inside the outlines on the page in the workbook, while you watch to ensure correct letter formation. As the learners write each letter, they should say the sound.
2. Read the instruction to the learners. Explain that the robot is a word-making robot – you feed it letters and it makes them into words. The learners' task is to predict which word the robot will make. The learners will find this task easier to begin with if you can give them some plastic or wooden letters to manipulate, so that they can explore combinations of letters. Alternatively, allow them to try writing out the letters on a whiteboard or piece of scrap paper. Show the learners that each box of letters is numbered. They need to write their answer in the empty box with the same number on the opposite side of the sheet. Model working through the first of the words and show the learners where the answer is written. Give them time to work through the rest of the page independently. Note that the first letter for each word is underlined in the left-hand column. Make sure learners then blend the sounds to read the words to check their spellings are correct.
3. Introduce this short story. Establish the expectation that the learners will read it aloud. They should be able to read all of the words in the story.
4. The last panel is left blank for them to draw their own picture to illustrate the end of the story. Ask the learners to read the last sentence carefully and decide what they think the picture should show. In some instances, they are invited to draw their own ending to the story.
5. This panel is used to introduce common, sometimes tricky words that cannot be read using phonics alone. Read the word aloud for the learners. Ask them to write it. Each time they finish writing the word over the letters shown in the workbook, ask them to say the word aloud. Explain that you want them to re-read the story, looking for these words. Each time they see one of these words, they should make a mark in the box under the word.

Phonics Workbook A

Teaching using template 6

Template 6 is used as follows:

Page numbers	Phonics focus	Words to look out for
22–23	Look back	cat, pin, peg, sun, dog, mop
42–43	ie, oa	goat, tie, soap, road, lie, goal, boat, pie, coat
44	oo, oo (long and short)	boot, book, foot, wood, moon, roof, wool, spoon, kangaroo

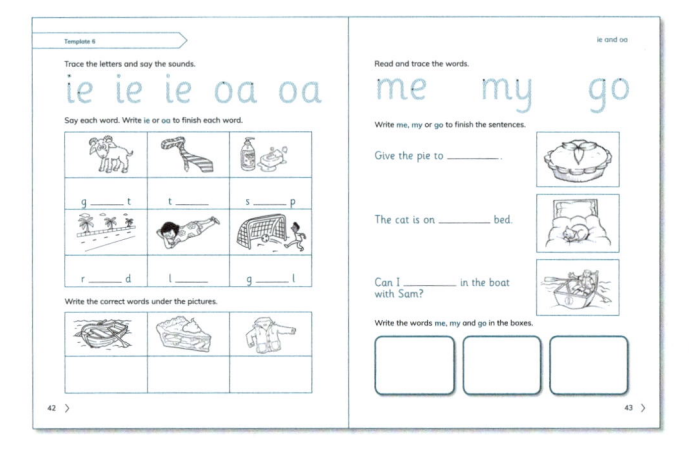

Teaching sequence

1 Say the sounds aloud and ask learners to repeat them with you. Although combinations of letters may be new, the letters themselves should be familiar. Learners should then trace the letter inside the outlines on the page in the workbook, while you watch to ensure correct letter formation. As they finish each letter or set of letters, ask them to tell you what sound the letter(s) represent(s).

2 Read the instruction to the learners. Ask them to identify the pictures. Encourage them to tell you the sounds in each word as they use 'phonic fingers' to show each sound. If appropriate, remind the learners that some sounds are made using more than one letter. Support the learners as they use their phonics fingers to help them to think about each sound as they write it to spell the words. Encourage them to say the sounds right through the word, rather than blending just the first two. For example, not **tr-i-p** but **t-r-i-p** learners should put up four fingers.

3 Read the instruction to the learners. Ask them to follow the instructions, write the words in the relevant box and be prepared to read the words back to you.

4 This panel is used to introduce common, sometimes tricky words that cannot be read using phonics alone. Read the words to the learners and talk about the letters in them. Ask them to trace the letters in the workbook and say the words. Warn them that they will need to remember the words for the reading activity.

5 Read the instruction to the learners. Page 23: Learners answer the questions with a ✓ (yes) or a ✗ (no). Page 43: Learners complete the questions with the most appropriate word.